Beyond the Night

Beyond the Night

A Remembrance

WAYNE GREENHAW

Black Belt Press
Montgomery

Black Belt Press

P.O. Box 551

Montgomery, AL 36101

Copyright © 1999 by Wayne Greenhaw.
All rights reserved under International and Pan-
American Copyright Conventions. Published in
the United States by Black Belt Press, an imprint
of Black Belt Publishing, LLC, Montgomery,
Alabama.

ISBN 1-880216-68-X

Printed in the United States of America by the
Maple-Vail Book Manufacturing Group

Illustrations on pages 7 and 9 by Steve Garst

First Printing

*The Black Belt, defined by its dark, rich soil,
stretches across central Alabama. It was the
heart of the cotton belt. It was and is a place
of great beauty, of extreme wealth and
grinding poverty, of pain and joy. Here we
take our stand, listening to the past, looking
to the future.*

For my sister-in-law, Julia,
her husband, Drennen,
and their son, Renn,
very special people.

Virtue: one of the orders of angels; right moral goodness; right action and thinking; uprightness; rectitude; morality; a particular moral quality regarded as good or meritorious, as, the *virtue* of generosity; specifically, in philosophy and theology, any of the cardinal virtues; also, excellence in general; merit; value; chastity, especially in a woman; effective power or force; efficacy; potency; especially, the ability to heal or strengthen; as, the *virtue* of medicine; bravery; valor; courage; daring; a mighty work; a miracle; *theological virtues;* the three virtues: faith, hope and charity; *to make a virtue of necessity:* to do what one has to do as if from inclination or a sense of duty.

— Webster's Third New International Dictionary

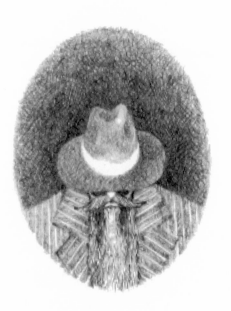

One

We lived in a brick ranch-style house on a shady street in a small town in north-central Alabama where everybody knew his neighbors.

When Daddy came home on Friday afternoons, after a week on the road selling barber-and-beauty supplies to shops across three southern states, our little black shaggy Cocker Spaniel named Midnight knew before the rest of us. He sensed Daddy's arrival before we heard the tires crunch up the gravel driveway.

We were playing in the backyard where Drake Glenn and Charlie Marks and I had built a hideout from scrap lumber, old cardboard from boxes Daddy's merchandise was shipped in, and roofing we picked up in the street after the tornado swept through last spring, barely missing our house but ripping to shreds Preacher Grant's parsonage. Drake was talking ninety-to-nothing about how we ought to give up cowboys-and-Indians and start playing cops-and-robbers. He was as serious as a Thanksgiving blessing, but Charlie kept throwing in, "Who's going to be the robbers?" upsetting Drake and causing him to lose his train of thought.

Midnight, who had been sitting in the corner listening to us, his eyes shutting from time to time, showing his boredom, perked his ears, turned his head slightly, and took off with an understated yelp. As his barks became more frantic, I heard the unmistakable sound of Daddy's Studebaker with its two little bouncy jitters before puffing to a stop.

After Daddy had kissed Mama and dumped his dirty clothes in the hamper, we sat around the kitchen listening to him tell about his week on the road. One time a year or so ago he told about meeting Hopalong Cassidy on the sidewalk in downtown Enterprise. My younger brother, Donnie Lee, asked Daddy a dozen questions about Hopalong. I could see Daddy making up answers like he knew the cowboy movie star's entire history frontways and backwards.

Daddy was a storyteller. Using his imagination, he made

the road the most fascinating place in the universe. When he came home from a week on the road, he always had a tale to tell. Sometimes more than one.

Another time he told about running smack into Lash LaRue, the cowboy who dressed in black and carried a bullwhip. He was mine and Donnie Lee's all-time favorite, and as Daddy told about him whipping out his leather weapon just in time to trip up a trio of outlaws robbing the First National Bank of Dozier, Donnie Lee and I were sitting on the edges of our chairs, hanging on to every word that squeezed out around Daddy's bobbing Kool cigarette.

This time, Daddy told about meeting an old man driving the backroads of the United States in his two-year-old Chevrolet. "He was about six-foot-three. Skinny as a rail. Had a scraggly salt-and-pepper beard. And when he talked, his voice sounded like silver."

"Silver?" Donnie Lee asked. He liked the world to make perfect sense and he couldn't put silver with the tone of a man's voice.

"Soft and shrill at once," Daddy said. "And bright. It was like polished silver. Like that that's worn bright in your pocket."

"Oh," Donnie Lee said, like it was clear as ice water.

Mama smiled while she put a hen in a roasting pan and

began sifting salt and pepper over the yellow skin.

"A bunch of us salesmen staying at the Waller Hotel were sitting around the lobby after supper. The old boys were telling jokes they'd heard in Mississippi and Georgia, and in walked this bearded gentleman dressed in a suit that looked like Chicago nineteen twenty eight."

Donnie Lee's face scrunched into a frown. "What's that look like?" he asked.

"Gray with little narrow dark stripes every inch or so."

"Oh."

"Wide lapels and padded shoulders. He looked like a Humphrey Bogart gangster movie."

"And he was in Greenville?" I asked.

"At the Waller Hotel. Had on a wide-brimmed hat the same shade of gray as the suit. Fine hat with a curled wide brim."

"Was he packing a pistol?" Donnie Lee asked.

"No," Daddy said. "But he sported a smile big as sunshine."

Mama smiled again as she slid the chicken into the hot oven.

Daddy leaned slightly toward us. His forehead wrinkled. His eyes held a bright sense of urgency. "This man came around to us and shook our hands. He acted like he'd known us a hundred years. Had something nice to say about each and every one of us."

"You aren't a hundred years old," Donnie Lee said.

Daddy smiled. "No, I'm not. But I feel like it sometimes. But this man made me feel like I was young again. There was a look of promise in his eyes."

"You're not young," Donnie Lee stated.

Mama chuckled and put her hand on Daddy's broad back. "Yes he is, Donnie Lee."

"No, ma'am," he said. "He's not."

Daddy also laughed.

"How'd he make you feel young?" I asked.

"He started talking to us about what we were doing, standing in front of us in that gabardine suit, shining like a star. He said, 'You know, you're in the world's greatest profession. To be able to go out into the world and talk to people and sell them something they need, that's a pure blessing.' His voice lilted, like a song," Daddy said. He almost closed his eyes, remembering.

"His voice sounded like he was singing a melody, full round notes whistling through his lips. You know how I told you about seeing Frank Sinatra at the Paramount in New York during the War? When I was in the Service?"

I nodded. It was one of my favorite stories, when Daddy

15

remembered times he was in the Army during World War II.

"Well, his voice was like Frank Sinatra singing a song. Other people have said the same words before, but when you hear a master expressing himself, you never think about the others. He's saying it the way it should be said. You listen so intently, your ears become more and more acute to the sound and the way it's being sung."

"You can hear better?"

"That's right," Daddy said. "It's like you can hear more than just the words."

"More than the words?" Donnie Lee asked.

"Like it's music," I said.

"That's right," Daddy said. "His voice takes on a new meaning because he's absolutely sincere. You know he's speaking to you from somewhere down deep."

"Like a preacher," Mama said. She always liked for us to know about preachers and preaching, The Bible and its stories. She'd said several times that it would be a wonderful thing in this world if I became a preacher when I grow up, but I had my doubts.

"What's the man's name?" Donnie Lee asked.

Daddy's hands opened at his chest. "Now, hold on a minute. Don't take me too fast. I want to tell it the way it happened, the way it truly happened."

Donnie Lee and I nodded.

Mama's hands remained on Daddy's back.

"He singled me out, saying to me, 'Harold,' he said, 'you're particularly lucky.'"

"How?" Donnie Lee asked.

Daddy's eyes pinched slightly. "I'll tell you."

We were all quiet, waiting.

"He said, 'You get to go out here in the countryside and sell folks things that make 'em look more presentable, even pretty, making their outsides glow with what they got on the inside.' And, you know, he made me think about my own self and my job, my line of work, so to speak. His words cut right to the heart of the matter, things I reckon I should of thought about but never had. I've got all that time between towns, driving those ribbons of asphalt from Gordo to Columbus to Starkville to Meridian to Frisco City and beyond. I've got all that time, but I've never done much down-right thinking about what I'm doing, like it had some deeper meaning. Not the way this stranger was talking it."

He hesitated.

Mama pulled out a chair and sat and watched him. We all listened. I thought we might be listening to him the way he listened to the man in the lobby at Greenville.

"He carried on about how we were the chosen profession. He said that traveling salesmen carry goodwill to remote parts of the world, like Greenville, Alabama. Bill Gray from Tallahassee said he'd been trying to tell his wife that for years. We had a little laugh. The man laughed with us. But it was no joke to him.

"He rared back and gazed into the face of each of us — one at a time — and got our undivided attention. 'You know what it's like to be out here in the lonely. That's what the open road is, you know. I know it. I've driven that Chevrolet 22,000-plus miles in the last couple of years, after I got back from the South Pacific, where I served in the Marines on Okinawa.'"

"What's that?" Donnie Lee asked.

"An island," I said.

"The U.S. Marines fought the Japanese army on that island and other islands. Every time we whipped them, we moved closer and closer to Japan, finally defeating them. You'll learn all about that in history or geography. But that's where he said he'd been. Then he said he'd moved around the U.S. seeing people and talking to people. Said he wanted to know all these folks he'd been fighting for."

"What'd he sell?" I asked.

"Nothing," Daddy said.

"How's he make a living?" Donnie Lee asked.

"He spreads happiness," Daddy said.

"Is he Santa Claus?" Donnie Lee asked. "You said he had a beard."

"Not as white as Santa Claus. It was speckled gray. He was a gray man, shaded with splotches of shadow."

"And Daddy said he was skinny," I said.

"I bet he was a preacher," Mama said.

"Kind of," Daddy said. "Yes, he was kind of a preacher. That night he piled all of us into his Chevy and rode us out of town."

"Weren't you scared?" Donnie Lee asked.

Daddy shook his head. "There was nothing about him that frightened us. We immediately liked him, trusted him and would travel anywhere he wanted us to go. It was like he was offering us something, with his hand extended."

We waited for the next words to fall.

"We first stopped at a super market on the edge of town and bought a box of groceries. Bread, baloney, mayonnaise, Vienna sausage, eggs, bacon, coffee, cans of all kinds of vegetables. We put that in the trunk of the man's car and off we went again. Out a ways in the pure darkness, he turned off the highway and took us down a dirt road. We found three shacks where five families lived all piled on top of one another. No electricity. No running water. No indoor plumbing. It was a shame anybody lives like that. The man said these poor Negro folks had been left to take care of themselves by the man who owned the property where they lived. He just left them there, said he'd be back, and they haven't seen him since. Winter's coming on. They had depleted their garden, except for a dozen or so stalks of collards. And you know what?"

"What?" Donnie Lee asked.

"Even in all their poverty, they asked if we'd come into their houses and have supper with them. They had some corn laid back and the women had made some pones of hoecake and had a big black pot simmering on a potbellied stove. And that pot was filled with collard greens.

"It smelled strong, but good. It really did. But we didn't go inside. We sat on the porch with them in the moonlight. The man told them that all these salesmen had pitched in and bought them groceries so they wouldn't go hungry during the next week. One little bitty woman who was as black as the stove grabbed hold of me and hugged me and pulled me close to her bony little ol' body. When she grinned she showed snaggled teeth and gums badly in need of a dentist. But she was so happy, I hugged her back and held her to me for a long moment, feeling her backbone under my palms. Her hair smelled of lye-soap."

"Oh, Harold," Mama said sweetly. To us, she said, "Your Daddy is such a good man."

"We were all good that night," he said. "We were all better than we usually are, because the man made us that way. He gave us extra feelings. He made us want to reach out.

"He told us we needed to look in the mirror more," Daddy said. "'Examine yourselves,' he told us. He left us sitting there in the lobby of that little hotel. At around midnight, he went outside and got in the Chevrolet and drove away. All of us guys smiled at each other and said, 'He was something, wasn't he?' and I said, 'Sure enough. You ever see him before?' and they all said they hadn't. Roy Blalock said, 'I hope we run into him again out here on the road in the lonely.' And Charlie Carr said, 'I doubt we will, but he is an experience, ain't he?' And we all agreed that it was indeed an experience."

To Mama, he said, "That night I slept better than I had in years. I slept right through the night without getting up once. I woke up so refreshed I thought I'd already taken my shower."

"Did you bathe?" Donnie Lee asked.

"Sure, I bathed. But I was washed deeper than soap could scrub. When I brushed my teeth and combed my hair, my body shone like a new penny. I swear, when I looked at myself in the mirror in that little bathroom, I glowed."

"Oh, honey," Mama said, then she touched his arm in a loving gesture.

"I sold more on my first three stops than I'd sold all the rest of the week. That night it took me twice as long to fill out my orders and send them in to the home office. But when I got through, I wasn't tired at all. My shoulders didn't ache or sag. I was in Selma that night at the Albert Hotel and Peeokle the bellman had a supper ready for me to eat in my room. Peeokle's wife had fixed pork roast, rice, gravy, stringbeans, and biscuits that melted in my mouth. When I finished, Peeokle just came right out and asked if I'd like to go down to the river and meet his wife and family. I knew him before the war and I've known him for three years since the war, and I never knew anything about his family. He's this short fat Negro man with a round jovial face. I always say, 'Howdy,' to him and he speaks back, both of us being friendly, but he'd never had me any special food or anything like that. We never made an effort with one another."

"We met him when we went with you last summer," I said.

"Yes, you did."

"He's a nice man," Donnie Lee said.

"Right again," Daddy said. "And he asked about y'all. I told him all about you. Then I went down there next to the

Alabama River on this curving narrow dirt lane, and I met his wife Alma and their three boys, Joeena, Peeokle Jr., and Raylander. They're six, four, and two."

"Which one's six?" Donnie Lee asked. He was six-and-a-half.

"Joeena," Daddy said. He spelled it.

"Funny name."

"It was the name of Peeokle's granddaddy who was a slave on a plantation down in the Black Belt. He was born into slavery down there before the beginning of the Civil War. His mama and daddy got sold away, and he was left in the care of his grandmother, until she died."

Donnie Lee, with a frown covering his round face, said, "They sold his mama and daddy?"

Daddy nodded solemnly. "They did that sometimes," he said.

"And the little boy didn't have any parents?" Donnie Lee asked.

"People are cruel sometimes," Daddy said.

Donnie Lee, still frowning, nodded.

"Peeokle was a little bitty thing and can't remember what his mama or daddy looked like. He got his name because his grandmother, who didn't have teeth and couldn't say 'pickle,' thought Peeokle looked like a little bitty pickled cucumber when he was a baby. And Alma, she's the daughter of a preacher from Uniontown, said she wanted to become a beautician."

"She did?" Mama asked.

"She said she thought she could fix women's hair in their neighborhood if she had the right machines to help her do the work."

"What'd you tell her?" Mama asked.

"I had picked up this old trade-in from a shop in Camden, and I took it out of my trunk and installed it for her right there in their living room. Peeokle and all of his three boys watched while I showed Alma how to turn it on. I gave her some new rollers and put out some permanent wave lotion."

"Don't colored folks do their hair different?" Mama said.

"I reckon they do," Daddy said. "But she'll have something to work with."

"You gave it to her?"

"Peeokle and Alma will pay me little by little, a few dollars next time I'm down that way, and I'll bring 'em more stuff."

"What's the company going to say?" Mama asked.

"Well . . ."

"Were you Santa Claus?" Again, that little sharp edge tinged Mama's words.

"No, ma'am. Not as much as the next night."

"What'd you do?"

"I fixed up a man named Theodus who lives in a voodoo shack on the west side of Montgomery."

"You fixed him up?"

"One of my regular customers, a barber named Smokey Robinson who runs a shop in the Jefferson Davis Hotel where the singer Hank Williams gets his hair cut, told me about this old Negro man named Theodus. He used to take care of me when he was a bellhop at the Whitley Hotel down there. Well, it seemed that Theodus wanted to open up a barber shop out in the quarters."

"And you . . ."

"I fixed him up."

"For a little bit every time you're down that way? Do you have a written contract?"

"No," Daddy said. He didn't continue.

"What's the company going to say?"

"They're not going to know."

"They'll know sooner or later. They'll say you're stealing from them."

Daddy chuckled again. "No, they're not. All of this came straight out of my pocket."

"Your pocket?" Mama said.

"Yes, ma'am."

"You mean, out of your children's pockets? That's really what you mean, isn't it? You know we don't have money to throw around. We can barely make ends meet. Since I stopped working, when Donnie Lee was born, it's been tough. But you don't care about that, do you?"

"Now, honey . . ."

"Don't 'now, honey' me." She pushed back her chair and stood.

"Baby, it's just a little . . ."

"You think you can sweet-talk me," Mama said as she bent over and opened the oven door and peeked inside. We heard a sizzling sound, and the aroma of the cooking chicken escaped and filled the little room.

"It sure smells good," Daddy said. He glanced toward us and said, "Boys, your Mama can sure-enough cook up a storm."

Later we ate the wonderful chicken, but neither Mama nor Daddy said much. He was through with his story. Donnie Lee and I both knew better than to ask more about the mysterious man from the hotel lobby in Greenville.

Two

On Saturday night we were getting ready for supper. Donnie Lee and I had played hard in the town park with our friends. The sun had shone bright and warm for a December afternoon. Daddy had gone into Birmingham, twenty-something miles to the west, to check in with his home office on First Avenue North. It was a place crowded with barber-and-beauty-shop merchandise, fresh with perfumy smells, heavy with paste and cardboard, alive with commerce — even on Saturdays.

After Daddy returned late that afternoon and we'd come

home from the touch football game, Mama baked cookies for a church sale that would take place after Sunday night prayer meeting. Midnight, waiting patiently for suppertime, was sprawled on the kitchen floor and watched Mama take the cookies from the oven. We were all washed and shiny when the phone rang.

Mama answered, then uttered, "Oh, no!" her voice catching in her throat. The receiver shook slightly in her hand as she listened. A moment later, her lips trembling, she handed the phone to Daddy.

She crumpled into a chair and reached out and took me and Donnie Lee in the crook of each arm. "Boys," she managed. She cleared her throat. She blinked her eyes but tears came anyway.

"It's your Paw-Paw," she said. Then whispered, barely audible, "He died a little while ago."

Midnight moaned in his throat and pushed his head against my leg, and I reached down and scratched behind his ears.

"Yes," Daddy said into the phone. "Yes. Did he . . ."

After a while Daddy hung up and turned to us. "Let's eat a bite, then start north."

Mama hugged us and kissed our damp cheeks. With a curled finger, she wiped the tears from Donnie Lee's freckled face. She patted our backs and said, "Y'all eat and I'll pack our bags."

Less than an hour later we headed out of our little town in the crowded Studebaker that smelled of bay rum and permanent wave lotion and the smoke from Daddy's Kools. Midnight's leash was snapped to the clothesline in the backyard, where he could run back and forth. I put his food and water bowls near, and our next-door neighbor promised to watch after him while we were gone.

Bundled up in the back seat, we were asleep before we climbed the first hill outside of town. When I kicked in my sleep, Donnie Lee grumbled something unintelligible. I poked him with the toe of my shoe and he swung his arm toward me and said, "Stop it! Daddy, tell him to stop it!"

Mama half-turned in the front seat and swatted her palm toward us and said, "Both of you stop it. Your Daddy doesn't want to hear you now."

Donnie Lee hit me again.

"Mama," I said. "Make Donnie Lee stop."

"Hush!" she said, and reached around and slapped me across my upper legs.

"Mama!" I said.

"Just hush! The both of you! Your Daddy's tired, and he's hurting. He doesn't want to listen to your foolishness."

I straightened up in the seat. I stared out the fogged back window into the cold of the night. Going through north Birmingham, I heard the sound of steel mills wheezing in the distance. With Daddy's window rolled down, sucking on his Kools one after the other, like these would be the last of a very long line of cigarettes, I smelled the harsh ugly stench of pig iron cooking. There had been times when we drove in on First Avenue North and stared over the concrete railing of the viaduct, down into Sloss Furnace, where the iron was so hot it flowed as a yellow liquid into forms that molded it into the shapes of small pigs. Miners dug ore from the hills surrounding Birmingham, trains brought it here to the mills, where its consistency was changed, then the bars were molded to be shipped north to make steel for manufacturing. That was the world into which I was born and around which I lived. I knew it only superficially, but I smelled it often enough to feel a strong kinship with its rhythm and its flavor.

Now and then, beyond Birmingham, we passed lights from a farmhouse and I wondered if a little boy and his brother and his father and mother lived there. I was glad we no longer lived on a farm. It was all right for a while. But Granddaddy kept wanting me to do more and more chores as I grew older. A farm is quiet and slow, and its rhythm drags to the point of boredom.

I glanced in the rearview mirror and saw the reflection of Daddy's face with tears streaming down from both eyes. I started to say something, but the words caught in my throat. Got to act like a big boy, I told myself, hearing Mama's voice in my mind.

Staring out into the nighttime world, I thought about the stranger in the lobby of the hotel in Greenville, a town not much larger than the one where we lived, only it was down in south Alabama in the middle of Piney Woods country. I wondered where the stranger came from and what he had truly given to Daddy and the other traveling salesmen. It had been something, I could tell. Whatever it was made Mama mad. But she didn't seem mad now. She was distraught over Paw-Paw, Daddy's father, whom I suddenly pictured in my mind: a big man with shoulders wider than Daddy's, a strong leathery face with deep-set eyes and a bushy brown mustache that tickled when he kissed hello and goodbye. Sometimes he held me in his broad lap and fixed his big hands on my shoulders and let me nuzzle my head between his shoulder and neck. He always smelled of strong rich pipe tobacco, the way Daddy smelled of Kools.

As usual, Daddy cut off the main north-and-south highway and took us on the road that wound around curves, circled huge rock boulders and a gigantic oak that was said

31

to be the oldest tree in the state of Alabama, dipped down to cross streams on narrow, sagging bridges, and lifted up over large wooded hills where my great-grandfather had settled before the turn of the century after his brother remained north of the great Tennessee River in the place called Athens in Limestone County. I liked the forest. It was different. It was a special place. Dark. Foreboding. Daddy always told stories about the forest. I liked it especially in the late afternoons, when we left our home in Trussville after lunch and drove through north Birmingham and turned into the forest while the sun was high in the west. Daddy said that outlaws once rode these hills. "The bank-robber Rube Burrow and his gang had their hideout in caves up here on the other side of Empire," Daddy'd say. "Rube Burrow was a whole lot meaner and more famous than Jesse James in these parts."

We had heard of Frank and Jesse James, had witnessed their exploits in Saturday afternoon movies, and knew they were hardened criminals worthy of their reputations. "Rube Burrow robbed trains that traveled across north Alabama, then he and his boys rode down here and disappeared into the thickness of the Bankhead Forest." When I looked out the car windows during the day, the forest closed in around us, becoming thicker and thicker the farther north Daddy drove. The trees became taller and grew closer together, cutting out most of the light, making it near dark down here on the ground. This was a mysterious place that evoked wild thoughts. It made my imagination skip across hills and valleys of wonder.

I cleared a hole in the foggy window and squinted as I looked out at the dark objects we passed in the night. When Daddy slowed for a tight curve and a steep dropoff, I saw the frightened eyes of a tiny deer. He looked back at me, and I figured he was wondering who I was and where I was going.

As Daddy turned the steering wheel, keeping us on our side of the road, getting ready to head down Penitentiary Mountain, suddenly a truck rolled out of a logging road. Daddy slammed on the brakes and we slid sideways down the steep highway slick with midnight fog. "Damn!" Daddy exclaimed under his breath.

"Boys!" Mama said. "Hang on!"

And Donnie Lee cried out in the darkness, "Mama!"

I grabbed hold of my brother and held him tightly, trying to cover his body with my own.

The car careened into the side of the truck, sending the Studebaker into a spin out of control, and Daddy worked fast to turn the wheel in the opposite direction. Then our car spun around in a circle and hit something else. That fast, the movement stopped. I felt myself being shot like a bullet out of the window and through the air. The world went around and around. My head whizzed upward. Tree limbs tore at my body. Leaves fluttered like a bird's wings. A violent pain ripped through my side and I landed hard, like a heavy rock being thrown.

When I opened my eyes, I looked around. I tried to utter "Mama," but the word caught in my dry throat and would not be said. The big full moon was as bright as a huge silver dollar. I heard something above my head. I rolled my eyes upward and looked into two big brown eyes. I gasped. A deer's narrow little face was no more than two feet away, looking at me with inquisitive eyes, a twist of the head, the hint of a smile playing on its lips.

"Where am I?" I asked. I started to rise but something heavy and hard hit my brain like a hammer. I went dizzy and lowered my head to the moss-covered rock pillow.

My body heavy and immobile, I lay very still and wondered where Mama and Daddy and Donnie Lee had gone. I tried to reconstruct what had happened. We were driving through Bankhead Forest in north Alabama. The forest wall had grown thicker and thicker, darker and darker, and I remembered seeing the deer and wondered if it was the same one that stood over me now and watched me.

We had been heading north toward Paw-Paw's. Then it hit me: he was dead. Mama had said he had walked downtown to the post office in Town Creek, the little cotton-gin town in the middle of the Tennessee River valley. On his way home, Paw-Paw had fallen. By the time the doctor got to him, he had stopped breathing. Maw-Maw said he suffered a heart attack.

We had been riding along quietly. Donnie Lee was sleeping with his snoring sound easing between his lips. When I sat up, a truck pulled out in front of us. Daddy worked the steering wheel one way, then the other. The car twisted around like a bumper car at the State Fair. There was a quick, hard, loud sound. Then all movement stopped with a thud.

I clinched my eyes shut, trying to think what happened after that, but no memory came to me. With my eyes clamped shut, my body was surrounded by cool, clear, still air. Everything had been washed clean. My body was fresh, like I had just stepped from the bath.

I was washed anew. I had heard Granddaddy, Mama's daddy over in Tuscaloosa, talk about being washed in the blood of the lamb, and I wondered if it had happened to me. He said that when you are saved you go through a transformation of the spirit. Religion came on you as quickly as the lightning that struck Saul on the way to Damascus. He was blinded, and when he awakened, he was a new person.

I did not smell of Ivory soap. My world now had a fragrance not unlike honeysuckle, mixed with early spring azalea and dogwood. But it wasn't spring. It was winter. December. In three weeks Santa Claus would be coming. It was cold.

But I wasn't cold. I was perfectly comfortable. I had a blanket pulled to my chin, but there was no one around to have put it there. Mama wasn't here. I didn't hear her. I didn't see her. She had always been with me, but now. . .

A soft velvet touched my cheek. I opened my eyes and stared into the animal's eyes. Its nose rubbed next to my skin.

"Deer," I whispered.

The head went up. Although it was a young deer, the curve of its neck from breast to chin was held at a regal angle. If it became a buck, it would be a great stag with a strong head and alert ears.

No sooner than I thought it, at the top of a hill across a narrow brook that babbled and bubbled over rocks and fallen limbs, a gigantic white-breasted buck with antlers silhouetted against the gray sky gazed toward us.

The small deer scampered across a carpet of leaves, leaping the stream, stumbling and nearly falling as it hit the other side, and scrambled awkwardly up the hill toward the stag. I knew how he felt: caught in a moment of weakness by his father, who was much older and very wise. And now he wanted to show that he could jump as high, run as fast, and climb as high as any full-grown deer.

In the shadows at the top of the hill the stag did not move as the youngster rushed to his side. The elder deer stood as still as a statue, head high and proud, breathing smoky fog through his nostrils, his back rigid, his legs anchored to the precipice. As the little one nuzzled against his side, he reached down and touched it with his nose. He shoved it easily and showed teeth with which he nipped it on the shoulder.

The fawn did a quick little dance, shrugged its body, then lowered its head in deference to the older, bigger deer.

As the first touch of sunlight twinkled through the still-damp pine needles of the tallest pines, the stag gave a faint toss of his head and let out a grumbling belch from his thick throat, like a primeval beast calling out to all the forest. Then, with a quick nudge against the little one, he kicked a rock and bounded down the far side away from me.

As the light expanded, a twittering of birds filled the woods like a million-member chorus. Bluebirds, cardinals, sparrows, and others danced from limb to limb. They looked at me and away, and I soon forgot my headache.

A pair of raccoons tiptoed to the edge of the water without noticing me. Fascinated, I watched as each dipped front paws into the chilly stream, then proceeded to wash their faces, their heads, and under each of their lifted front legs.

When I made the slightest move, they stopped. Their paws uplifted, they held their pose and twisted their heads in my direction and regarded me with hooded eyes, like two bandits stopping by the wayside during a run for freedom. When I did not make another move, they backed across the shallow stream, keeping their heads cocked in my direction. As soon as they were on dry land again, they broke and ran. Their paws barely touched the ground as they trotted up the hillside and disappeared.

In their place came two chipmunks, gnawing constantly with their front teeth, digging beneath the layer of dry leaves, picking at the rich black dirt, making an early breakfast of roots and herbs. When they spied me, they burrowed into the ground and vanished beneath the leaves. One retreated and peeked out and studied me, then he turned and dug into the ground again, not willing to trust me.

Afterward, when the birds became more active, I sat up again. This time my head did not send alarm messages through my body. I blinked my eyes.

I felt around my body. Nothing seemed broken. I was sore in the ribcage, but not so much that I couldn't push and pull myself to a standing position. One elbow was skinned, already turning blue-black under the rough red skin. A bump rose on my forehead but when I checked my fingers I saw no blood. Otherwise, I was okay.

I remembered crashing through the window of the car. Or I thought I did. I had grabbed Donnie Lee. I held him close. I wanted to protect him. I didn't want any harm to come to my brother.

"Donnie Lee?" I said aloud. My throat, my lips, my voice worked fine. "Donnie Lee?" I asked again, louder. There was no answer.

If I held him tightly in the car, where could he be? I looked behind several trees and the big rock boulder. *Where is the car?*

A red fox crawled from beneath a rock ledge above the creek. Standing in a wedge of early morning sunlight, his coat glimmered like a colt's. His head came to a point like a dark red diamond. His eyes burned in that royal head as he stared in my direction. He sniffed the air, shook his head, and walked off nonchalantly, showing me without question that he was not in the least bit afraid of my presence. This was his domain.

Using a crooked fallen tree limb as my walking stick, I pushed up to the crest of the hill. The road had to be close. I could not have been thrown a far distance. Somewhere up ahead, I would find Mama and Daddy and Donnie Lee.

At the top I looked out over more woods. Then I surveyed in the opposite direction. I discovered more woods.

I found a rock the perfect size and sat on it and contemplated my predicament. *Where is the road?* I tried to think it out logically.

Then I circled around the top of the hill. With each circle, the circumference grew larger and larger. I reasoned that soon I would find them—or at least the place where the accident occurred—if I continued to hunt in such a methodical manner. If I found the road, a car would come by soon. They would find me.

Before long, I wished I had put a cookie in my pocket or a piece of candy. After the fourth circle, I pictured a sausage and biscuit in my mind. I thought about early mornings at Maw-Maw's, when she fed me hot oatmeal with butter melting in the center and cream on the side. When she first put it on the table when I was a little boy, I didn't like it. *Why put something cold on something hot?* I asked myself. After I tried it and sweetened it with a spoonful of sugar and mixed it all up real good, I put it to my mouth and wondered on how good it was. It wasn't like breakfast at Nanny's house. Mama's mother usually had fried eggs and grits and smoked ham with red-eye gravy, or seasoned-with-sage-and-pepper sausage with big doughy biscuits. At the moment, however, with the cool fresh fragrance of the forest filling my lungs, I prayed for a big platter heaping with anything. A bowl of oatmeal or one biscuit would be a treasure.

As I tromped through the underbrush–mossy ferns of various shapes and sizes, green leaves almost as tall as me, mountain laurel growing near the trunks of trees–I soon interrupted two squirrels playing tag. They stopped, looked at me, glanced at each other, and skittered quickly up a tree. I laughed, thinking they looked like me and Donnie Lee in our backyard, where we sometimes played rough-and-tumble, slapping each other on the butt, running, one tackling the other. Sometimes I'd get too rough and he would fall and skin his knee or hit his head, and he'd jump up and run screaming into the house. I wanted to bash him hard when he did that, but it was never long before we were at it again. We were like the squirrels, playing and playing–and we didn't like strangers interfering with our make-believe games.

Late in the morning, tired and hungry, after filling my stomach twice with water from the stream I had crossed four or five times, I sat on a downed tree trunk. The magnificent tree had been chopped in two with an axe. Then the branches had been trimmed and used for a bonfire. I found the small black ring where the fire had burned. The hikers or hunters or campers did not cover the fire with dirt and leaves, the way we were taught in Boy Scouts. They just left it open, obviously not caring what it did to the forest. There were signs of only two or three people, cutting down a tree that had taken hundreds of years to grow. I couldn't reach half-way around the tree's trunk. I looked at the place where the axe had bitten into the wood. I wondered why people would go to so much trouble, just for one night of camping, just to build one fire, or perhaps two, if they stayed for breakfast. I wondered.

Beyond the remnants of the fire was a hole. Next to it were three empty cans. Raccoons or squirrels or some other critter had dug them up and had licked them clean. Kicking one, I wished I had a can of pork-'n-beans or even a cold can of tomato soup. My stomach growled. I thought about some of the curse words Daddy sometimes used, and I brought up damn, and I damned the campers for not digging the hole deeper for their garbage. *If this keeps happening, I thought, pretty soon Donnie Lee and I won't have a forest to camp out in when we grow up.*

I knew that the sun rose in the east and set in the west. I judged the main highway was to the east. If I walked in that direction, sooner or later I would find civilization.

I headed out.

As I stepped to the top of a rounded hill I saw something a hundred feet ahead quickly disappear behind the largest tree in the hollow. Several ridges, like natural furrows following the contours of the hill, were all covered with layer upon layer of dried and rotting leaves, providing a natural compost. Granddaddy Able had told me about such. He'd shown me the way nature cared for itself. He said, "It's God's plan: things build naturally." Then he pointed out how he had to make furrows to keep his field from washing away with the first hard spring rain. "The furrow holds the water back, allows it to flow from side to side, and gives us a walking path between soybeans and vegetables and fruit trees and corn," he said. That was the way of his people, the farmers of southwest Ireland, the country where his grandfather had been raised, where his father had planted fields and grown crops before him, clearing rocks from the rolling hills and plowing and planting and harvesting right down to the cliff that dropped to the ocean.

Here, deep in the forest, nature was doing the same thing without the benefit of thought-out plans or a history of one man passing knowledge down from generation to generation. Here was the earth doing for itself according to God's unwritten plan. It was just happening.

As I headed around the crest of the hill that curved to the south and back east, I looked up through the curtain of tree-tops, seeing bits and pieces of clear blue sky as the breeze from below became warmer. I pulled out of my prized blue windbreaker and tied the arms around my waist. *Somewhere out here,* I thought, *I'll find them.*

I trudged ahead. The more I walked, the less the wounds of the crash hurt. With each step my body healed itself. As it healed, however, the more my stomach cried out for something to eat.

Thinking back about how the chipmunks and wood-chucks foraged for roots, at the far end of the hill I climbed down into the next dark hollow.

Near a trickling stream, I bent down and raked back the leaves and dug into the black earth. Using my fingers as a tool, I scooped a handful and brought it up. It smelled rich and sweet. No person had ever touched it, and I felt almost guilty for having disturbed this piece of dirt.

In several more diggings, I discovered several small roots running sideways away from a small bush. With extra effort, I tore it away. When I had six pieces about five-inches long, I took them to the stream and washed them in the cold water. Then I put one into my mouth and began to chew. The flavor was not the most delicious, but the juice from the root filtered through my mouth and down my throat. Its sweet-sour taste was far better than nothing.

Later, after I filled the hole and pushed the leaves to cover the place where I had dug, I sat back and looked around. Squirrels played in a far tree. Birds flickered from branch to branch. An army of grasshoppers jumped in unison across the tops of dry leaves.

I spotted a berry bush twenty feet away. I wondered why I had not seen it before, but I hadn't. I picked a handful, smelled them, and pinched into one. A gooey red substance smeared across my finger. It had no particular smell. I touched my tongue to it and tasted a tart flavor and decided it was better than the roots. I ate the entire handful, then I started on my way again.

By the time the mid-day sun brightened, even in December, I was hot. I stripped off my tee-shirt and crammed it into one of my back pockets.

I came upon a ridge high above the world. I sat on a rock ledge and looked down, across the tops of oaks and sycamore and hickory and pine. Below, a small river ran through a three-hundred-foot-deep canyon. I was on top of a rock wall just like the one five hundred feet across from me. Suddenly my stomach began to growl. I felt a cramp catch inside my belly. A foul-tasting bile worked its way up my throat. Something inside my belly turned a flip-flop. I leaned over and let a dark red liquid erupt from my insides. I spat and spat, trying to rid myself of the foul taste.

After my stomach eased, I wiped my mouth with the tee-shirt, put it back on, climbed down to the river and washed my mouth with the water there.

I found a meandering path over rocks that did not drop in a straight wall. I lowered myself from bush to bush, holding to sturdy little plants, using them like a climber's rope. By the time I reached the bank of the river I was so tired I collapsed on a bed of pine needles and leaves. I managed to crawl to the water and cup a handful and suck the liquid down my throat. Then I lay back and closed my eyes. Momentarily I was asleep and dreaming about playing in our backyard with Donnie Lee. I was the outlaw Rube Burrow and he was the sheriff searching for me. I was holed up in my hideout with my six-shooter strapped around my shoulder in the style of a Mexican bandito. When we talked among ourselves about the outlaws, Drake Glenn and Donnie Lee and I decided this band of crooks was different from all others. They had been born and raised in northeast Alabama, no more than fifty miles as the crow flies from Paw-Paw and Maw-Maw's house in Town Creek, but they were very much like the Mexican bad guys we saw in the John Wayne and

Tom Mix and Hopalong Cassidy movies on Saturday at the picture show in Homewood. That's where Mama or Daddy dropped us at ten a.m. with a dollar in our pockets, leaving us to see a double-feature and three serials, and picking us up at two p.m. to head back to Trussville, where we would trace the action of the movie once again, assigning various roles to our home-town actors.

When I awakened, the first thing I saw was a hawk with a five-foot wing-span soaring high in the eggshell-blue sky. The hawk made circles the way I had walked in circles. Now and then he urged himself forward with a flap of his wings, then he floated, legs and talon tucked, head outstretched, a picture of quiet power.

After a while I noticed he was dropping lower and lower with each new circle. His eyes bore down on mine, and I rose and moved into the shade. The hawk was interested in me. He wanted to see what kind of prey I made. *Did I look like dinner?* Suddenly my mouth went dry and sour again. My throat was parched. I knelt next to the stream and dunked my face into the water and sucked. I pulled the water inside so fast I choked. I jerked my head up and spat the water out. I coughed twice and spat again. I reached down and cupped the water and brought it up to my lips. This time it went down with ease.

I sat on the bank and contemplated the water. It was not real deep here. Not over my head. I saw fish swimming in the shallows. I remembered having read about Indians wading into streams and reaching down and grabbing a fish.

To do this, I would have to pull off my clothes and wade into the water. While it was not over my head, it was at least waist-deep. I decided to find shallower water. I started walking downstream. I thought I might find a bridge. If a highway ran over the river, I would follow it. *Surely I can't be that far from civilization,* I thought.

When our car hit the truck and whatever else, we were only a half-hour north of Double Springs, which was no metropolis, but at least a thousand people lived there. I had heard Daddy talk about the bootleggers in these hills. They had to live somewhere.

Daddy's grandfathers on both sides lived in the forest. Way before the turn of the century, Jonathan Motts Greenhaw shook his brother's hand about fifteen miles north of the Tennessee River. Lawrence Morgan Greenhaw, the younger brother, decided he would put down roots in what was to become Limestone County. A year or so later he met a young woman whom he courted and married and started raising a family in that rich cotton land. Jonathan made it across the mighty Tennessee River, traveled for a good day and a half

48

until the land started to rise again. On the crest of the first large hill he put down his goods and tied his two mules to a tree. He cleared forty acres, planted an orchard, drank from a nearby spring, and met a young woman from a yonder hillside, courted her, and brought her to his new home. Years later, my Paw-Paw and Maw-Maw moved to flat land, a place Daddy had pointed out hundreds of times at the foot of Penitentiary Mountain. In a hummock of oaks and sycamores they built a log house with a dog-trot through the middle and started a family that grew to fifteen children, three of whom died before they were a month old. Twelve survived. Paw-Paw and Maw-Maw, John Wesley and Martha Susan Montgomery Greenhaw, moved their brood twenty-some-odd miles northwest to Town Creek, where he grew cotton and vegetables, and made sure that nine of the twelve siblings received college educations. My father, Harold, the youngest and the most rebellious, snubbed his nose at college and made his way as a traveling salesman. "It's what I know," I'd heard him say many times. "I love people and like to be among them. I talk their language. As long as I've got something they need and want, I'll earn a decent wage." He told me more than once that he actually enjoyed paying taxes to the government. "That way," he said, "I know I'm making something, and it's a good investment in the future for you and your brother." I thought that if more people believed the way he did, our country would be stronger and more solid from the foundation to the top of the roof.

As I walked along the riverbank, I kept my eyes peeled for anything I might eat, for a shallow place, and for the site of an old home place.

I heard it before I saw it. Water rippled with a gurgling sound. I quickened my pace. It could not be far ahead. Its sound was like the joyful noise of children giggling.

I was stepping on the balls of my feet when I spotted the rapids bubbling up, spilling over rocks, falling over pebbles, bouncing.

I rushed to it and sat on a large rock and pulled off my shoes and socks and britches. There was a three-inch tear in the seat of my pants. I even pulled off my underwear and shirt.

Naked, I waded out into the shallow but quick-flowing rapids.

The cold water lapped against my ankles. It grew quickly deeper. I worked at staying up on the largest rocks. With the tips of my fingers to steady me, I moved from one spot to the next, like a blind person.

At a place where the water flowed with the greatest velocity, I lowered myself. When I was thigh-deep, I slipped. I fell sideways, the bottom of my right foot sliding against a slick rock. I grabbed out. My fingers reached for a big rock. I grasped, but they wouldn't hold. I slid back and downward. In a moment, I was chest-deep, and I breathed heavily, the water chilling my entire body. I shivered. Then I quickly lowered all but my head into the cold water.

Ahead, a foot-long brown-green fish swam away from me. I had no idea what kind it was: a trout, I thought, but it didn't matter. I reached toward it.

The fish twisted its body and propelled through the water with such speed that my hands slapped together.

A moment later another fish came into sight. I tried to position my body in front of it. I would tackle it, like a lineman in football. The fish zigzagged, and my whole body tumbled forward and fell into the river.

I moved downstream into slower-moving water. Two fish swam together, moving from side to side like they were dancing a slow waltz. Again, I managed to step in front of them, thinking they would swim into my hands. I held my hands in front of my body. I reached for them as fast as I could move. With seemingly no effort at all, they slid past me.

I stood straight up in the water. Naked as a jaybird, I looked around at the woods, the trees and the rocks, the birds that flew from tree to tree, the animals hidden somewhere beyond the first layer of growth, and suddenly I laughed loudly. "You silly fool," I called out to myself and anyone else who might be listening.

I worked my way back upstream. Several more times I tried to grab a fish, Indian-style. I didn't even come close. Once, I thought I felt the side of a fish's slick scales, but the feeling was probably in my imagination.

I climbed out of the water and sat on the rock and let the last warm sunshine of the afternoon dry my body.

Thirty minutes later I put on my clothes. Then I set out to find a place that would be warm and dry when the cool night air started to blow. I asked myself where an animal would go.

I continued on my way, following the river northeastward. I remembered seeing a story in *The Birmingham News* several weeks ago about college students running the rapids of the West Sipsey Fork in canoes. I did not know what this river was called, but the high rocky bluffs rising a hundred feet up from the banks on each side, the twisting downward fall of the water, and the thick stand of trees that came up to the edges fit the pictures that went along with the Sunday sports article in *The News*.

Near the highest bluff, I found in the growing darkness a well-worn path. I followed it through the thick trees along the riverbank to a place that looked as though it had been a campsite. Again I saw the ring of black where a fire had burned. I searched the area and found thick packed pine straw beneath a rock ledge. Strangers had slept here. Someone had made a mattress from the straw and never swept it out into the wilderness when they had finished using it. I was thankful for their absent-mindedness or their carelessness.

As I curled up in the straw, I became acutely aware of the rumbling in my stomach. I wondered how long I could go without eating, especially since the berries had made me sick and emptied my stomach.

I wished I had been wearing my heavy winter coat instead of the thin windbreaker. By the darkest part of night, the cold stung my skin. I breathed thick fog. I covered my mouth and breathed into my hands, and later I lay on top of my hands and arms.

My entire body quivered as my predicament worked its way through my mind. I had never been so alone in my life. I had no idea where I was or how to find my way back home. I was colder than I had ever been — even when it snowed winter before last. The thought of never seeing Mama or Daddy or Donnie Lee or Midnight again hit me and made me shiver and feel even colder. I shut my eyes tight and began to pray. I remembered the words. I mumbled, "The Lord is my shepherd, I shall not want. He maketh me to lie down in green pastures. He restoreth my soul. Yea though I walk through the valley . . ."

Soon after falling asleep in pure exhaustion, I awakened with my entire body shivering. I turned in the straw and curled into an even tighter ball, scrunching my backside against the dirt under the rock ledge.

Then I heard a movement. I froze. *What is it?* I thought. I thought it so loud, I wondered if I actually said the words. If I had, I was in trouble.

What could possibly be more trouble? I asked myself. Then I saw something move about twenty feet away. I asked myself the first question again. My insides rumbled again.

I tightened my grip on myself just as I recognized the outline of a bear in the moonlight. He seemed as big as the largest Kodiak I had read about in *National Geographic*. At that moment I would have sworn he was fifteen feet tall and weighed a ton. Actually, when he came closer, he was a small black bear no more than four feet high and weighed about fifty pounds. But I was no less afraid. My pulse raced. My heartbeat was loud and strong. I did not move an inch.

That quickly, the thoughts of freezing vanished.

I thought that perhaps the bear would search the campsite. Finding nothing, he would move on. Perhaps this was his regular nightly routine. But I was not so lucky. No more than ten feet away, he sat down on his haunches and started picking at the place where the fire had been. It made me think once again that campers had been here recently — perhaps even last night, although it would have been a terrible time to go camping. Still, the bear was interested and kept at his work.

Moments later he stomped around, slamming his paws down against the dirt. On the far side of the clearing, he stopped. Again, he sat back on his rear. He grunted three or four times, then began digging.

Within moments, he unearthed a sack. Tin hit against tin. I smelled something that reeked of sardines. The hint of cheese flavored the air. Then another odor caught my nostrils.

I was so hungry, I even forgot the fear that had filled me with trepidation. *What the heck,* I was larger than the bear. If I had to . . .

I rolled from beneath the ledge. I leaped to my feet. As loud as I could shout, I screamed, "Aaaaiiii!" like a banshee or a wild Indian. The bear jumped to his back feet. He too let out a scream. A sound of fright or madness eked from his throat, his mouth thrown open, teeth exposed. Just when I thought he was about to rush me, as I ran madly toward him, he took off down the pathway and disappeared into the woods.

I went directly to the sack.

With far more delight than the bear had displayed, I threw open the bag and began exploring its contents. I discovered an unopened can of sardines and almost cut my fingers as I ripped the metal key from the underside, slipped it into the slot on top, and peeled back the tin cover. When some of the juice spilled, I sucked it from my fingers and my stomach rumbled its thankful acknowledgment. I dug out every delectable taste, smacked it with my lips, savored it with my tongue, and chewed it long and carefully. God, it was good, and I had never before liked sardines. When Daddy had gotten sardines and crackers at a country store, I always turned away in disgust; *how could anyone eat little sour-smelling fish?* From this moment on, sardines would always be a treat.

I found a half-eaten can of potted meat, another food item I had always turned up my nose at; but now I ate every smidgen. Three saltine crackers were left in its wax-paper wrapper. I nibbled them to nothing.

When I finished off half of someone's leftover moon pie, I surveyed all the containers to make sure I had not missed anything. Then I crawled back under the ledge, covered myself with the straw and was asleep in less than a minute.

Three

Again, I awakened at first light. I blinked. The vision of the black bear filled my mind. I shivered with the fright of remembering. *How stupid could I have been?*

My hunger had overcome logic. I walked back to the river and, after washing out my mouth and drinking, I sat and tried to think how to continue my search for a way out of the forest.

Surely, I thought, they must be looking for me by now. But the only sign of mankind had been the signs of fire and the half-buried provisions the campers had left behind. Silently I thanked them for their wasteful and sloppy behavior. No one who admired and courted nature and used its beauty should treat it so haphazardly. But at the moment I was glad they had.

I followed the river eastward, moving upstream, and an hour later I saw a bridge in the distance. I stopped, took another drink of water, felt my spirits renewed, then headed toward it. The closer I got, the clearer I saw that it was not the kind of bridge I was seeking. It was a wooden expanse. Still, where there was a bridge there had to be a road. Closer, I saw that it was a long covered bridge with crisscrosses of dark wood beneath a tin roof. It had been here for a long long while. Thick trusses came down at angles from under the bridge to hold it steady as it crossed the deep gorge. I climbed a zigzag path hikers had made up the side of the steep dirt-and-rock wall above the northern bank of the river.

I did not stop until I was at the top, out of breath, and tired. I sat at the end of the bridge and scanned its length, like staring through a cave that opened two-hundred feet away. Sunlight poured through the latticework on the eastern side and through holes in the roof, where pieces of tin had blown off or fallen. I stepped gingerly onto the bridge and walked uneasily for twelve steps. The old boards creaked under my feet. When I made two more steps, the ancient timber rocked sideways slightly. I grabbed a hold on one of the four-by-fours that had been a part of the original bracing. I imagined that it had once been a very sturdy construction. But it had long since given way to natural and manmade elements of destruction. About twenty more feet toward the middle, I noticed a place where someone had built a fire. Beer cans and potato chip bags, wadded brown sacks, an old brown banana peel and an empty whiskey bottle lay, strewn around another blackened charred circle — this one in the wood of the floor of the bridge, where it could have easily burned down the entire structure. A pair of women's underpants hung, showing off a streak of devil-be-damned behavior as it waved in the breeze from a rafter.

As I moved back toward the side where I had entered, I stepped quickly, not wanting to become another destructive force against this monument to another time. There had once been a well-worn road leading to the bridge but now it was only two ruts grown over with weeds and wildflowers. Less than a half-mile into the woods it vanished into nature. I searched for a place where it might pick up, knowing that the fire and other debris came from people who traveled here from somewhere. But apparently they had not come down this road.

I followed what might have been the road. Now and then

there was a rut. Trees grew in relatively straight rows. Still, I couldn't be certain. Nevertheless, I persisted through the morning.

I saw the signs of animals. Squirrels played in distant trees. They stopped momentarily and watched me pass. Then they continued their scampering after I walked by.

When I saw an old rusted tin can, I knew I was getting close to something that might be modern-day civilization. It wasn't a hundred years old. That was for sure.

I kicked the can and heard its flat sound as it tumbled across the top of bitterweeds and fell into a hole.

I wondered how long it would take for the earth to be covered by old tin cans if people kept throwing them out along the sides of highways throughout my life. I was just a little boy. Already I saw cans and bottles and boxes and paper strewn across the landscape of my life. Even out here, where nature was supposed to rule over the animals, the plants, the geological twists and turns of the earth, a horrible mess was being made.

At the top of a long but gradual climb I found an open meadow covered with sage grass yellow as gold, bending slightly with a breeze from the northwest. In the middle of the field were a half-dozen water oaks, each with limbs that stretched a hundred feet, forming a perfect shaded circle. This was an old home place. Daddy had pointed out such places along the highway between our house and Tuscaloosa, where Granddaddy and Nanny lived, and our house and Town Creek, where Maw-Maw and Paw-Paw had lived. It looked cool and inviting, a place where once upon a time a house had been standing in the middle of the hummock of trees.

As I neared I saw several stacks of bricks of a foundation. On the far side was the remains of a chimney, a fireplace opened to the interior of the ghost house. The road that had disappeared halfway up the hill had run nearby, on its way to somewhere, and the house would have faced the road.

I walked over the remaining brick steps and imagined a living room, a parlor, a hall, bedrooms, and in the back the ground was charred black as soot where the kitchen had been. I figured that the fire had probably started there and spread to the rest of the building.

I kicked through the place before I sat on one of the stacks of bricks and enjoyed the cool breeze that whistled lightly through the darkening shadows of the trees. I breathed deeply the cool pine-fresh air that filtered through the tall long-leaf pines from the far edge of the forest beyond the sage field.

I smelled something that made me look around the kitchen, searching the ground. A few minutes later I found a wide wooden door flat with the surface of the earth. I reached down and twisted an old metal handle. I pulled. It didn't budge.

I pulled again. I used all of my strength to squeeze it open. Holding it several feet up, I gazed down into the black chasm of the opening. I smelled the fresh water and the limestone earth through which the hole had been dug.

I pulled it the rest of the way open, stood back and looked around the area.In a pile of debris under the shaded area I found a galvanized pitcher and ladle. I laid them aside and kicked through planks, some rusted tin utensils, bedsprings that creaked when I stood on them, and, when I moved a piece of linoleum to one side, found a ball of rope. I fished it out and unrolled it and stretched it, testing its strength against my pull. Satisfied, I tied one end to the pitcher, which I lowered into the darkness of the well. Less than ten feet down, I heard the metal container splash into water. I let it down several more inches, felt it grow heavy against my hold, and then lifted it.

Water was splashing out the lip when I grabbed it and steadied it. Away from the opening, I ran my hand around the inside of the pitcher to wash away the dust of its years of sitting here.

With it halfway clean, I lowered it again and drew it up. I put my lips to the rim and sucked the cool clear fresh-tasting water into my mouth and down my throat. Finished, I sat back. Where the water had spilled down the front of my shirt, the breeze was cooler.

Tired and bone-weary, I lay down on a bed of thick sage grass I fashioned for myself in the sunlight. I coupled my fingers behind my head and stared up into the azure sky. I closed my eyes and fell into a deep sleep within moments.

When I awakened, the sky was dark. Lightning flashed through clouds to the north. Thunder rumbled. A drop of rain hit me on the forehead.

I moved under the trees quickly. Guarded from the rain, I backed close to the trunk of the largest water oak. I wrapped my arms around my knees that folded against my chest. I put my cheek next to my upper legs and prayed as hard as I had last night. When I closed my eyes, I pictured Mama standing on the front stoop of our three-bedroom two-bath brick ranch-style home in Trussville, a place she had said was "perfect" when we first moved there three years ago. Daddy stood next to her in his lightweight navy-blue suit, the trousers pleated, the coat double-breasted with wide lapels, the tie also blue with touches of red and white zigzagging over the four-inch wide silk. Daddy was grinning as he sometimes does when he is enormously happy. His right hand is resting on Donnie Lee's right shoulder, where his fingers are caressing my younger brother in a loving fatherly way. Next to Donnie Lee's right leg stands Midnight, who also looks happy. I squeezed my eyes shut stronger but could not find an image of me. I was missing.

Tears welled up behind my eyes, and as hard as I tried not to, I cried and cried. Each time I opened and closed my eyes, tears flowed. My body shook. I was so torn in two, I didn't mind the drops of rain that made it through the limbs and leaves and leaked onto my head. I squeezed my knees tighter, trying to keep from shivering relentlessly. I knew it wasn't from the wet or the cold. It was from the lonesome nothingness that surrounded me and captured me and held me hostage here in someone else's home place. It was from thinking that I would never see my family again, and I missed them, and I wondered how they felt about me. Maybe they were going on with whatever life they had without me. I filled only a small void. I had never done anything. Not really. I had accomplished nothing. I was just a kid. I lived and had my friends. I wondered what Drake Glenn and the others at Trussville Elementary were doing this moment. *Were they missing me?* Maybe they were having a devotional about me, bowing their heads in a moment of silent prayer. Maybe Brother Elliott at Trussville Baptist was saying a prayer to the whole congregation, asking them to pray for me at night and in the morning. *It was Sunday, wasn't it?* I couldn't even re-member. How many days and nights have I been out here?

The rain poured. Thunder rocked the heavens. A piece of lightning broke through a cloud and cracked like a rod of steel snapping in two. My body tensed tighter than before. Another lightning bolt shot down. Far across the field, heaven's electricity jolted through the top of a large tree. A limb broke. A stream of smoke rose from the naked wood. Half the tree tumbled and dropped. Then, beyond the rhythm of the rain against the leaves overhead, the world was silent.

When the rain finally stopped and everything around me was washed clean, the sage grass smelling gamy, the newly wet earth opening my nostrils with its damp sweetness, the trees shaking the settled rain from its leaves in a rush of wind, like a dog after a dousing, I wiped my eyes and sniffed my nose and stood and walked out beyond the big trees. Along a furrow I found two dozen apple trees loaded with fruit. I picked a red-splotched apple and bit into it and chewed its liquid sweetness, the juice running around the corners of my mouth, where I licked the sticky sweet. I picked two more and went back to the oaks and the well. I hung my jacket over a low-lying limb like I belonged here. I dipped another good drink from the well and found a relatively dry spot and sat there and ate slowly. I felt like a king with a feast.

Since I had food and water and a tree for shelter, I stayed in the meadow. I wandered out to the edge, looking for more fruit trees and anything else a farmer might have planted when he and his family lived here. I discovered more trees, but these were fruitless. Several peach trees had died and withered. At the northeastern corner of the clearing a scrawny patch of berries filled an indentation in the ground. I lowered myself into it and picked. I let five of the berries rest in my mouth before chomping them. Each tiny bubble burst as my teeth cracked it open, each exploding with a sweetness, like purple sugar. Between bites, I filled two pockets and carried them back with me to the trees. As I emptied my pockets I smiled at the way the berries had stained my pants. I knew that if Mama was here she would scold me and carry on about having to wash my clothes three times a week just to keep me in something clean. She'd make me shuck out of my clothes right now and demand that I stand here while she washed them.

With the thought of her, tears tried to form again. But I chased them away. *I'll live,* I told myself.

Then it dawned on me that they might not have lived. If the wreck threw me only-the-Lord-knew-how-far from the car, what happened to them? Maybe, when I tried to wrap Donnie Lee's body close to my own, he hit something that would otherwise have hit me. Maybe in my anxious state of mind I had saved myself but had sacrificed him. *What if. . .*

My mind raced from one thought to another. I'll rest, I thought, *then I'll move on first thing tomorrow morning.*

Four

That night I saw a thousand stars. I lay on my sage-brush bed and stared up into the sky that reached its blackness from one end of the universe to the other. I immediately saw the dippers, the north star, then I picked out Orion the bear with all of its tiny dots clustered together to make the head, then those a million miles apart, then I recognized what I thought was Mars and perhaps Saturn. I had forgotten there were so many stars, and each and every one was so bright out here. It was different from in town or even in our backyard at Trussville. It was even different from Granddaddy and

Nanny's. Once when I had been visiting Maw-Maw and Paw-Paw a cousin and I borrowed ponies and rode to the Saunders Mansion, a great yellow-brick castle towering over a cluster of oak trees even larger than this one, and we spent the night camped in the yard of the Mansion that had not been occupied since before the turn of the century. Aunt Lucy had told us the castle was haunted by two sisters who had been widowed in the Civil War and died here of old age and loneliness. That night, scared and remembering the stories Aunt Lucy had told us about how the sisters were murdered by slaves they refused to emancipate, we found solace in the stars. That night near the Saunders Mansion had shown me more stars than I had ever seen at one sitting. Looking up, I felt tiny. *Compared to all that, what are we?* I asked.

Although I had listened intently to lessons in Sunday school, had talked with Brother Elliott about the power of God, I had never actually come to a conclusion within myself. But if a boy sits beneath an oak and listens to the roar of thunder and sees a lightning bolt flicker through a dark sky and hears the crashing sound as it hits a tree, breaking a hundred-year-old sycamore in half like a matchstick, then he knows something more than he knew an instant earlier.

Thinking such thoughts, dwelling on the fact that I was learning something new with every step I was taking through the forest, I drifted again into a deep sleep.

I was awakened by a melodious song from a bird in the tree. Loud and cheerful, the bird's breast swelled with air before he released a song that shrilled through chords like a golden flute, hitting notes so high only nature's instrument could reach them.

On this day, with a new vision in my head and my stomach packed with apples, my pockets filled with berries, I was off toward the north.

Before I reached the fourth hollow, I heard the rush of water. It was much louder than the rapids.

I moved up the hillside through the dense underbrush. I was heading in a new direction. A sudden confidence filled me. I had only to step forward and I would find them around the next tree, bend, over the next hill.

Standing on the top of the hill, I looked through the skeleton limbs of trees. Far down below, my vision cutting crosswise like the early morning sunlight, fresh and open, a waterfall poured from a triangle of rocks. This forest was so far away from everything else in my world: not at all like the planned and perfectly laid-out streets of Trussville. These hills and hollows were scattered here haphazardly, like they were the result of some kind of holy war. Thousands of gallons of water poured down over more than two hundred feet of rocky ledge, the water pounding downward without slowing, being sliced by sharp rocks, until at the bottom it bounced into a round pool of water. No motion picture producer could have placed it in a more perfect spot, and yet there was no one here to enjoy its separateness but me and the trio of bluebirds that dove down into the mist that sprayed near the pool. There, where the fog formed an invisible curtain, a rainbow curled upward red and yellow and green, as abstract as a modern painting, and yet so real I felt I could reach out and touch it.

I was a child who knew he was in the presence of a miracle, a transformation of real into my own strange fantasy. With a lighter step than normal, a mind free of worry, I strode into the sparkling new world without an instant's hesitation.

Suddenly, a path parted. Stepping stones as clean as Mama's kitchen floor provided an entrance. Sunlight streamed down through a cloudless sky. A warmth was like a blanket over my body. Next to the pool of clear water spread a bed of moss. I lay upon it and rolled sideways and looked down at the foot-long fish that swam in schools of six, gliding past me as though on parade.

I tasted the water transformed to icy lemonade as it touched my lips. I drank heartily.

I could not remember ever being so thoroughly refreshed.

My brain was soothed by the special massage of a light breeze, my slight muscles comforted by an infrared heat, my memory cleansed by the rainbow and the bluebirds.

The world was not like this. We learned in Sunday school that this is an imperfect place. Man can only seek perfection, knowing that he will never attain it. *But if this is not perfection . . .*

I lay back and closed my eyes. How could someone dream of some place better? How? What was the use?

A small deer like the fawn of my first day stood at the edge of the clearing and stared at me. His innocent eyes beckoned. His head was carried as haughtily as the stag's. His look was adoring.

I rose to my feet.

The deer stepped back, then to the side. The longer I watched, the more female its characteristics became.

"Wait," I said.

She moved very slowly, looking back over her shoulder in my direction, her face a picture of promise. She waited.

I stepped toward the graceful animal. Beyond the deer stood an arbor loaded with dark red grapes hanging in clusters. I gazed back at the waterfall and the pond and the fish and the bluebirds and the rainbow that looked as though it had been painted.

Then I turned and followed the deer, whose front legs were like a dancer's, long and slender with sinewy, string-like muscles stretched beautifully lithe toward her dainty hooves, delicate as she stepped beneath the arbor and vanished into the wilderness.

As though pulled by some force far beyond my control, my hand reached up to the first cluster of grapes. My fingers squeezed and pulled. I had to reach out quickly with my other hand to catch the fruit that snapped from the vine.

I looked beyond the arbor but did not see the deer. I saw only the woods from which I had come. All of the geography of the place ran together or folded over or doubled back, confusing me.

As my lips and teeth closed on the first grape, I looked back to see the waterfall and the rainbow and the pool, all slipping back into the distance. When my teeth bit into the skin and the soft sweetness burst into my mouth, all of the perfectly beautiful picture of the waterfall and the pool and the rainbow vanished. It became a simple hollow with a hillside path, a large pile of rocks, and a brook meandering through it. It was lovely, but it was not perfection.

I chewed the muscadine and swallowed it and tasted its fresh fine flavor settle down into my stomach.

When I reached for more grapes, the vine turned to kudzu

with big green leaves and no fruit. I searched beneath the leaves for more grapes, but all of them were gone. I stepped beyond the wall of the arbor and the dried leaves crackled under the weight of my feet. I was suddenly back in the same forest where I had been lost. I wandered northward and tried to remember the exact location of the waterfall and the pool and the rainbow. The farther I walked, the more the memory of that place and the warmth it emitted turned blurry and out of focus.

Late in the day I came to the conclusion that I was going around and around in circles. One hollow looked and felt like the one I had just passed through. I found a trickling stream. It barely had enough water to manage a handful. The taste of the wild grape had long since disappeared from my mouth. Once again, my stomach growled angrily and demanded food.

I sat on a rock at the edge of a clearing and bowed my head. Thoughts of Mama and Daddy and Donnie Lee forced tears from my eyes. I pictured them lying torn and mangled, bleeding with broken limbs, their own faces begging for help, with strangers milling all around them with no order whatsoever to their actions. I was in their midst, but I could do nothing. I tried to tell the men and women in white that these were my parents, my brother, that they were injured and needed help, but no one could hear me. I was there but I wasn't. I spoke but could not be heard. I cried out but no one listened. I screamed but my voice was muffled.

Then, at that very moment when the agony was so unbearable I was ready to reach inside my own body and tear out my heart to give it to someone for some reason, a stranger stepped out of the woods and stood in the shadows of a sycamore and smiled a snaggle-toothed grin. He was at once ugly and handsome. "What's wrong, partner? Life got you down?" he asked in a voice so slow and low I had a hard time picking it up.

He stood well over six-feet tall, was skinny as a scarecrow, had a scraggly gray beard that grew in splotches, thick at the chin, thin on the ruddy cheeks, and thick again near his large ears.

"It's a wonder you haven't starved to death out here in this wilderness," he said. Daddy said the stranger who appeared to him and the other salesmen had a voice like silver, and that was what I picked up from this man who looked at me with a growing sharpness in his steel blue eyes.

"You know my Daddy?" I asked, taking in his light gray shark-skin suit that reflected a brightness between the wide-set thin dark stripes.

"Sure I do," he answered. "I showed him things and told

him stories he'll never forget. They'll last beyond memory."

"How can a thing do that?" I asked.

"It ain't a *thing*, partner. It's a high lonesome feeling that carries through the wind from man to boy."

His voice lilted up like a song when you least expected it to, then it dropped. He sounded like an old cowboy from a picture show about driving cattle to a faraway town or a singer from a colorful riverboat dancing movie.

He had on a western-style hat that was the same shade of gray as his suit, and when he swept it off his head with his right hand he exposed thick gray hair matted with sweat. He dug a handkerchief from his back pocket and wiped it across his forehead.

"Too hot for a day in December," he said.

"The sun's been shining all morning," I commented. I didn't want to open up too much to this stranger, although he looked at me like he could see straight through my body and could tell me things about myself even I didn't know.

"Your Daddy's a friendly man," he said.

"He's a salesman," I said.

"I know," he said. "One of the best I've ever seen, and I've seen many a salesman in my day." He smiled lightly, his crooked teeth flashing. "And I've seen many days in many years."

I didn't say anything but looked down at the sharp silver toes of his shiny black boots.

"Like these boots, do you?" he asked.

"They're very nice."

"Made by the same artisan who fashioned Bat Masterson's for him. Said they'd last a lifetime." He grinned even stronger.

"That was a long time . . ."

"In Cheyenne, 1873. I traded him the buckle of a belt worn by David when he slew Goliath, and if you believe that little tale, I'll tell you another that's twice as long and three times as tall without the slightest hesitation." His words ran together better than President Roosevelt's in his fireside chats.

"You didn't . . ." I started.

"I did," he said, with a slight nod. "Thing of it is, you ask too many questions, like your Daddy and those other salesmen. But your Daddy is the best. He can talk the stink off a billygoat, and that's going a ways, I'm here to tell you. You got to listen to your old man, son. Too often you just dismiss what he says as just so much south Alabama hogwash, but I'm here to tell you, he knows a heap about which he talks. He would of made a good preacher, if that had been his calling."

"You a preacher?" I asked.

"Kinda," he said. "I move about the world in an old beat-up Chevrolet, talking to people of all trades, all sexes and all ages. If I was put here to speak only to grown-ups, how could I be here speaking with you?"

"I'm just a boy," I said.

"That you are, and a fine one too."

"I'm lost," I said.

"Not as much as you think," he said. "You're a young man who knows his way around this world."

"I am?"

"Of course, it's a small world."

"I feel lost."

"You are. You cried, didn't you? When you thought about your mother and father and little brother?"

"You know about them? Are they all right?"

"You're worried?"

"I always worry about them, when I don't know where they're at or what they're doing."

"Like when they've gone off to Birmingham and left you behind, playing baseball or something, and you get home before they do and sit on the back stoop and gaze at the lonely road."

"How'd you know . . ."

His smile flickered. "I know. It's a lonesome road, until

you see your Daddy's Studebaker coming from the direction of town, then it's a happy road."

I nodded.

"You really worry a lot about your little brother, don't you?"

I nodded again.

"He worries about you too."

"He does?"

"You didn't know?"

"I reckon not."

"You feel like you're the only one who worries."

I didn't say anything but looked at the deep wrinkles of his map-like face.

"They worry. All of 'em. They've been worrying about you."

"They're . . .?"

"They're fine."

"Are they in a hospital somewhere?"

"Yes, but they're fine."

"What's wrong with them?"

"You have to trust me."

"Why?"

"You're being as inquisitive as Donnie Lee."

I smiled. "You know him."

"He's an interesting person."

"Yes, he is," I agreed.

"Are you hungry?" he asked.

"I am," I said. I nodded, emphasizing my hunger.

He reached into his coat pocket and pulled out a small package and placed it in my palm.

I looked at the wrapping.

"It's something good to eat."

I unwrapped half of a bologna sandwich with lettuce, tomato, mayonnaise.

"I don't like mayonnaise," I said.

"No wonder you're hungry. I suppose you don't like apples and blackberries and herbs from the ground."

"If I have to eat it. . ."

He glanced toward the sandwich.

"I ate the other half," he said.

I bit into the sandwich and chewed, and it tasted better than I had ever imagined a sandwich tasting.

"See there," he said. "You're learning to be an adult and do things you don't always like to do."

"Is that what makes a person an adult?" I asked.

"It's one of the virtues of adulthood."

"A virtue," I mulled.

"That's correct," he drawled. He put his hat back onto

his head and cocked it slightly to the side.

"You look right handsome in that hat," I offered.

"Thank you, sir," he said. "Expressing yourself that way, you're displaying another virtue: of uprightness and rectitude."

"What's rectitude?"

"Being honest and making good judgments."

"I'm honest," I said.

"Yes, I think you are."

"I am."

"Would you like to find your way out of this place?"

"Yes."

"First you have to come with me."

I followed him into the deepest darkest part of the forest. The growth was thicker and heavier. As we walked down the pathway, leaves overhead guarded us from the sun. Then a layer of huge leaves the size of elephant ears covered those, until even the heaviest green turned near black. He held my hand as he led me down through an undergrowth like terrain from a Tarzan movie.

"Scared?" the long-legged man asked.

"Yes," I said.

"Good. You're afraid of the unknown. But you've been in the forest four days."

"Nothing like this," I said.

I felt his grip tighten on my hand as we circled the trunk of a huge tree. Overhead animals jumped from tree to tree. There were no monkeys in Alabama. These must have been squirrels or raccoons or possums. It could be cats. I had heard that wildcats lived in Alabama woods. Once in the third grade Billy Ingram's father brought the stuffed body of a spotted wildcat to our class and showed its long teeth, its mad snarling face, its furry paws and long sharp claws. Frozen on a piece of driftwood, the tiger-like wildcat sent chill bumps up my backbone. When I imagined coming face-to-face with such a creature, I shivered.

Halfway into the dark chasm of trees and undergrowth, I asked, "Where're we going?"

"Into the strange land."

"I've been in a strange country."

"Nothing like this," he said.

Suddenly a bright light flickered overhead.

I stopped as the light grew larger, shining upon us through an opening in the highest leaves of the trees nearly two-hundred feet above us.

"Come," he said, urging me on.

I hesitated, glancing upward, then moved to his command. The pathway was so brilliantly lighted I was almost blinded. I was guided by the touch of his hand. My insides quivered. My heart trembled.

Overhead, a sound started like thunder. Then it heightened. A wind blew from the northwest. Leaves rumbled like a freight train. A coldness swept over me and engulfed me, and I shivered more than I had in the cold naked morning of the first day.

"What is it?" I asked.

He did not answer.

We moved on slowly into the great dark room. At once I felt comforted and frightened as his steps slowed, and then he stopped. An instant later, he released my hand.

I tried to grab for him but could not find his fingers.

The light behind us went black.

I grasped my palms together at the bottom of my belly.

Out of the blind darkness came the flicker of movement. When I narrowed my eyes I saw something in the thick underbrush. It moved easily, not bothering to find a path but stepping onto the large leaves and pushing them to the ground, making them crackle under the weight. As my eyes adjusted, I saw a cat. He was big and black. His eyes shone like two twinkling yellow diamonds. He showed his teeth and growled deep in his throat.

On my other side I felt another movement. In that direction I saw a white tiger moving with the same graceful step as the first. He was the same size. Put them side-by-side and they would stand shoulder-to-shoulder. His head rocked from side to side, raking against the thick plants. He slowed. Seeing the other cat, he too bared his teeth. He growled even deeper, even meaner, even more intensely than the first.

Both stopped. I looked from one to the other.

I looked around for a place to hide, but I was totally exposed. There was no place to run.

Then, like that, the cats stepped toward each other. Their strides deliberate, they circled each other, the black intending to smell the white, who growled again and snapped a hiss, teeth cracking in the air.My insides caught, frozen as cold as ice.

The black twisted quickly, pivoted onto his hind legs, rose in the air, struck outward with his huge paw. His hateful cry shrieked, high-pitched and angry. His eyes flashed like fires burned in his head.

The white lowered his head and jerked it to the side. He dropped his shoulder and pushed it with all of his weight into the shoulder of the black.

With a paw still extended, the black slapped the white, hitting him across his hefty withers.

The white rolled over and came at the black from beneath. He grabbed with his two-inch teeth a mouthful of fur under the black's front right leg, then snatched it back with the whip of his head.

The black's growl lifted to an angry snarl. He jumped back. Then he lurched forward immediately, without hesitating half a second. He grasped the white's front leg in his mouth. He turned his entire chest and front body.

With the speed of a fingersnap, they rolled together in a great ball, both snarling and growling, biting and clawing.

I shook my head. I didn't know which I wanted to win. I knew I didn't want either or both to turn on me in their state of anger. They were so close I could smell their madness squeeze from their nostrils.

"Which shall it be?" the man asked, his voice as thin as a dime, with no concern.

"I don't know," I said.

"You have to know."

"But I don't. I don't know them. I've never seen them before."

"Do they have to have a history?" he asked.

"Of course," I said. "Everybody has a history."

"Even you?"

"Yes."

At that moment the cats broke away from each other.

They backed away, face looking angrily into face. Both showed teeth. Both growled. Then each turned and walked away in opposite directions.

"You saved one," the man said.

"Which?" I asked.

"Does it matter?"

"I don't know."

"As I said, you must know. You always should know."

"Why?"

"That's the law of the jungle."

"But this is not. . ."

"You don't know where you are, do you?"

Leaves above and in front of me opened. A light shone directly into my face. I was blinded. I squeezed my lids together. I put my hand up to shield my eyes. I saw nothing but the flash that held steady against my skin.

A voice asked, "You are Wayne?"

My lips trembled. I could barely squeeze the sound up and out of my throat. I finally managed to answer, "Yes."

I felt stupid. But I was captured. There was no escape. I could go nowhere. I was a prisoner. I was at this man's mercy.

But the voice did not come from the bearded man in the gray suit. I did not recognize the voice.

"Wha . . .what can I do?" I asked. The wind ceased. No

leaf nor limb stirred. Silence filled the entire below-the-earth world. Not even a bird moved. I sucked in my breath. As far as I could tell, the man who had brought me here was no longer with me. But I was not alone.

"Mister?" I whispered. It seemed as though my one word bounced off the trees and echoed around the place and ricocheted back into my eyes.

"You are alone," the voice said. It was a voice that evoked truth and sadness.

"I have no one," I said in my little boy's voice. It was the voice I used when Mama confronted me with something I had done wrong or when the teacher asked me about something I was not proud of doing. I wanted sympathy in the worse kind of way. I wanted to pull it from the very air. I wanted it to rush out from within.

"Alone," the voice said again. The word was heavy. It covered me with a new sadness. I thought about Mama and Daddy and Donnie Lee, about Maw-Maw and Paw-Paw, about Granddaddy and Nanny, and I thought about the man in the gray suit and wondered why he had brought me here.

I was about to become angry when the voice said, "You must prepare."

"For what?" I whispered. Even as low as I said it, the words magnified.

As quickly as my mind tried to picture my entire family, although Paw-Paw was dead and buried, my body rose up from the mossy path. I reached out for a nearby plant that was head-high. I did not want to rise. I wanted to stay on the ground.

A leaf tore from my hand.

This is crazy, I thought. *It's December, yet these plants are green. It's full wintertime, yet it is warm here. I am in the middle of the forest, and someone is playing tricks on me.*

I almost shouted, "I want my Mama," but I refrained at the very last frightening second.

In the still darkness, I was suspended above the plants of the undergrowth and away from the trees. I relaxed in a state of complete weightlessness. All of my aches from the wreck, all of the tiredness from the walking and climbing and lying on the floor of the woods, all of the hunger that had been gnawing at my stomach, any ill feeling whatsoever vanished as though it had been washed clean of my body. I was helpless, and I didn't care. I was suspended in mid-air, but I was not afraid of falling. In fact, all fear left me.

I flew upward through the hole in the trees, flying toward the bright light, but my eyes were not now blinded.

I turned on my side as I traveled through the air over the forest and a highway and high above a field where men were gathering bales of hay onto a flat-bed truck. I leveled out again as I swept above a small town where children were playing on a swing in someone's back yard. I waved but they didn't wave back. For a few miles I followed a highway, passing several cars, a truck and a school bus, then I sailed over a galvanized cotton gin and a big tin-roofed warehouse, and below I recognized Brackin's Drug Store and Callahan's Filling Station and Elmer Lee's Dry Goods and the new super market that was being built next to the east-west highway running from Decatur to the Tri-Cities. In front of me was Paw-Paw's house with the chinaberry tree where Donnie Lee and I climbed and played cowboys and Indians and the neatly mowed lawn over which we romped when we came here in the summertime. On the wide porch was Daddy sitting in a rockingchair and Maw-Maw on the canvas-covered glider and Aunt Lucy next to her. I didn't see Mama and Donnie Lee, and I wondered if they had been badly injured in the crash on the highway in the forest. I hovered overhead as Daddy glanced at his watch and said, "We'll have to get back to the hospital soon," and Mama came out the front door and said, "Donnie Lee will have to stay with Lillie Mae tonight," and Aunt Lucy said, "He can come back over here, if he'd like." I was shaken but relieved. I was not in the picture, and my absence left questions unanswered.

Just as I started to speak, my eyes opened and I looked up into the shadowy gray face of the stranger who had guided me into the darkness.

"What happened?" I asked.

"You were taking a close look at yourself and your world. We almost lost you there for a moment."

"Oh," I said.

I pushed myself up onto my elbows and gazed around. We were on the edge of a meadow. The man was kneeling over me. I did not see the black world into which we had climbed together.

"I'm hungry," I announced.

The man smiled. Regarding him closely, I saw the reason why he wore a gray beard. His skin was badly pocked, scarred from ear to ear and down along-side his neck. I started to ask him about it but held the words inside; that would be too rude, I decided. He smiled again, like he knew what I was thinking.

He put out his hand for me to hold. "Come with me, and I'll take you to get something to eat, then home."

At the far end of the meadow covered with golden sage we got into his old Chevrolet and rode down the highway off the mountain. "My great-grandfather and great-grandmother used to live up here on Penitentiary Mountain," I told him.

"Is that so?" he asked.

At the bottom of the hill at a place called Wren we stopped at a store next to a tiny cemetery. The proprietor said he had some fresh souse meat that had been made when the Montgomery family killed a hog last week.

"They're my cousins," I said.

"Is that right?"

Then I told him about my great-grandfather and great-grandmother, and he said, "I know the Greenhaw family. You know, that cemetery over yonder is the Montgomery Family Cemetery. They buried old John Greenhaw over there last week."

After we fixed slices of souse meat between soft pieces of lightbread, I guided the stranger into the graveyard. In the middle, among stones that marked Montgomerys and going back beyond the turn of the century, a new grave was cut into the thick grass with red dirt piled in a seven-by-four-foot rectangle.

"That's my Paw-Paw," I told the man, who nodded.

"Before you go any further," he said, "there's something I think a boy like you needs."

"What's that?" I asked.

He disappeared into the store and came out momentarily. He walked to me and handed me a small box. In the

Chevrolet, I opened it and looked down on a bone-handled Barlow knife with two blades. When I glanced over at him, the stranger said, "You handled yourself pretty well on your own, but a boy always needs a knife. No telling when you might need it."

"Yes, sir," I said, and I rubbed my palm over the rough edges of the real bone and knew I'd treasure it.

When I looked out the front window toward the highway, a truck three times bigger than the Chevrolet headed straight toward us. As it came closer and closer, I shut my eyes.

I awakened, screaming.

"It's all right, Son," a voice said. "You're okay." A firm warm hand touched my cheek. I stared into Daddy's face and shook my head.

"It was a big truck," I said.

"Not that big," he said. "But you were thrown a far piece."

I closed my eyes and shook my head. "Did I . . . " I started.

"You've been dreaming a long hard dream," Daddy said.

Mama appeared at the doorway. Her anxious face melted into a sweet happy look. "Wayne?" she said. "You've been out of it . . ."

"Paw-Paw died, Son," Daddy said as he wiped a cool damp rag over my forehead. "We buried him last week, while you were in the hospital here. The doctor says you'll be just fine."

"Buried him in the Montgomery Family Cemetery," I said.

"How'd you know?" Mama asked.

"I've always pointed it out to the boys," Daddy said. "Every time we pass there on the highway north of the forest."

I listened as they told me what all had happened over the past four days.

"I died," I said. "But I didn't go far."

"You what?" Mama said.

"They told you, 'We almost lost him.'"

"How'd you know that?"

I smiled. "I just do. My heart stopped. I stopped breathing."

"But you were . . ."

"You've been dreaming a lot," Daddy said. "I stood here and wiped a cool cloth over your forehead when the sweat broke and you talked deliriously."

I asked about Donnie Lee, who was outside wanting to come in to see me. And I asked about Midnight and was told our neighbors, the Bates, had fetched him and was keeping him in their backyard. They'd lost their dog last summer, and Milton and Peggy were giving Midnight the loving he needed, Mama said.

Daddy went on and on about how the doctor said I'd been delirious after I was brought to the hospital following the wreck. I had been in a feverish coma. When Daddy finished one of his speeches, I said, "Is my pants in the closet?"

Mama fetched them.

I dug my hand into my right front pocket and came out with a brand-new bone-handled Barlow knife.

"Where'd you get that?" Daddy asked.

"A man gave it to me," I said. "He said all boys need a knife."

Daddy frowned. "He's right," he said. "No telling when you might find yourself in the woods and in need of a knife."

I held the knife close to my chest that still hurt when I breathed deeply. I held it tightly and wondered.

About the Author

A native Alabamian, Wayne Greenhaw has written thirteen books and hundreds of articles. Named Travel Writer of the Year by the Southeastern Tourism Society in 1995, he writes regular travel features and book reviews for the *Mobile Register*. As a staff writer for *The Montgomery Advertiser* and *Alabama Journal*, he won numerous state, regional and national awards for his reporting and was a Nieman Fellow at Harvard in 1972-73. He studied in Mexico at the Instituto Allende in San Miguel de Allende, Guanajuato, and Mexico City College, and he graduated from the University of Alabama. He has been director of the Alabama Bureau of Tourism and Travel, editor and publisher of ALABAMA Magazine, associate publisher of Black Belt Publishing, and a teacher at several central Alabama universities. He lives in Montgomery with his wife, Circuit Judge Sally Greenhaw, and their terrier, Miss Priss.